··· A **TIMELINE HISTORY** OF THE ···

CALIFORNIA GOLD RUSH

·· **TIMELINE TRACKERS**: WESTWARD EXPANSION ···

STEPHANIE WATSON

Lerner Publications ◆ Minneapolis

CONTENTS

Lerner Publications Company
A division of Lerner Publishing Group, Inc.
241 First Avenue North
Minneapolis, MN 55401 USA

For reading levels and more information, look up this title at www.lernerbooks.com.

Library of Congress Cataloging-in-Publication Data

Watson, Stephanie, 1969–
    A timeline history of the California Gold Rush / by Stephanie Watson.
        pages cm. — (Timeline trackers: westward expansion)
    Includes index.
    Audience: Grades 4–6.
    ISBN 978-1-4677-8580-8 (lib. : alk. paper)
    ISBN 978-1-4677-8636-2 (pbk.)
    ISBN 978-1-4677-8637-9 (EB pdf)
    1. California—Gold discoveries—Juvenile literature. 2. California—Gold discoveries—Chronology—Juvenile literature. 3. California—History—1846–1850—Chronology—Juvenile literature. I. Title.
F865.W365 2015
979.4'04—dc23   2014041987

Manufactured in the United States of America
1 – BP – 7/15/15

COVER PHOTO:
Prospectors pan for gold during the California gold rush in 1849.

INTRODUCTION

In the mid-nineteenth century, most Americans thought of California as a wild, unknown place. Only a scattering of American Indians, Spanish and Mexican settlers, and American frontiersmen lived in its mountain valleys. A few whalers and merchants built settlements along its coast.

Then, in 1848, a carpenter named James Marshall made a glittering discovery in the Sacramento Valley. In the beds of rivers and streams that flowed from the Sierra Nevada were specks, flakes, and nuggets of gold.

News traveled fast. Gold fever quickly spread across the country and around the world. By the thousands, men left their homes, families, and jobs. Women began to travel to the West Coast as well but in far fewer numbers—one woman for every one hundred men. They were all bound for California. All these people wanted to stake their claim and strike it rich.

Finding a fortune wasn't easy. Panning for gold was backbreaking work. Some men did become very wealthy. Others returned home empty-handed. Conflicts arose during the rush for gold. Most American miners were wary of foreigners and American Indians.

In just seven years, the gold rush was over. Yet in that short time, it transformed California and the whole nation. Men who made their fortune in gold started businesses and built cities. People from many nations arrived to fill those cities. In their quest for gold, the prospectors clashed with American Indians and set the stage for long-lasting tensions.

The gold rush triggered the biggest migration in US history. It led to the construction of a cross-continental railroad. And though the California miners are long gone, their exploits launched a major turning point in American history.

TIMELINES

In this book, a series of dates and important events appear in timelines. Timelines are a visual way of showing a series of events over a time period. A timeline often reveals the cause and effect of events. It can help explain how one moment in history leads to the next. The timelines in this book display important turning points surrounding the California gold rush. Each timeline is marked with different intervals of time, depending on how close together events happened. Solid lines in the timelines indicate regular intervals of time. Dashed lines represent bigger jumps in time.

CHAPTER 1

AN UNKNOWN LAND

1500   **1700**   **1725**   **1750**

1542: Spain claims California as part of its colony.

1700s: The Spanish build forts and missions in California.

California is a land of contrasts. In the north are steep mountains, fertile valleys, and dense forests. Along the coast are sandy beaches lined with steep, rocky cliffs. And in the south are hot, dry deserts.

American Indians were the first people to live in California. For centuries they fished in its streams and hunted in its valleys. By the eighteenth century, California was home to two hundred different American Indian nations, including the Chumash, the Hupa, and the Pomo.

Spanish explorers had also started to notice the area's mild climate and rich farmlands. The Spanish began to explore California's coast in the sixteenth century and claimed California for the Spanish Empire in 1542. That empire stretched across the western and southern United States, Mexico, and Central America.

Dec. 29, 1845: Texas becomes part of the United States.

May 13, 1846: The Mexican-American War begins.

1822: California becomes part of Mexico.

1821: Mexico declares independence from Spain.

1775   1800   1825   1850

1836: Texas declares independence from Mexico.

Feb. 2, 1848: The war ends, and California becomes part of the United States.

Spanish explorers arrived in California in 1542.

It was called New Spain. An official called a viceroy ruled the area. He reported to the king of Spain.

In the eighteenth century, the Spanish began to colonize California. They built missions and military forts called presidios. The Spanish forced American Indians to work in these settlements.

By the early nineteenth century, native Mexican peoples, American Indians, and Creoles (Spaniards who had been born in the new country) had grown tired of Spanish rule. Mexicans wanted to take back the land they believed the Spanish had stolen from their ancestors. American Indians resented Spanish control of their homeland and wanted to be free from slave labor. Creoles did not like the new rules Spain had put in place to make the colony more modern. So they began to rebel. In 1810 the Creoles led a revolution against the Spanish. It was called the Mexican War of Independence. In 1821 Mexico declared its independence from Spain. A year later, California became part of the Mexican Empire.

Native Mexican peoples, American Indians, and Creoles fight Spanish colonists at Monte de las Cruces in 1810.

Soon afterward, Texas attempted to break free from Mexico and become its own country. In 1835 American colonists in Texas fought against the Mexican army and won. A year later, Texas declared itself independent of Mexico. And leaders in the United States became increasingly interested in the lands southwest of the US border.

New Lands in the West

In the early 1840s, America was made up of just twenty-six states. They stretched from the East Coast to Missouri. Florida, Iowa, and Wisconsin were territories. They were part of the United States but had not yet become states. The United States did not yet control much of the Midwest and the Northwest. What became known as the American Southwest was still part of Mexico.

When James K. Polk became president in 1845, he set his sights on the West. He knew Texas had rich farmland that could produce a bounty of crops. California had ports from which the United States could trade with countries across the Pacific Ocean. And he needed the land that later became New Mexico, Colorado, Utah, and Arizona to build a railroad that would connect the East and West Coasts.

James K. Polk

Lawmakers in the South had their own plans. They wanted to acquire new lands out west and expand slavery into those areas. But all of these lands were still under Mexico's control. In 1845 the Texan government asked the United States to annex Texas. The US government agreed. Yet Mexico did not recognize Texas's independence. When Texas was annexed, Mexico threatened war against the United States.

Mexico refused to give the United States any more land. But Polk would not give up his quest for expansion. On May 13, 1846, America declared war against Mexico. The war went on for two years. Then, on February 2, 1848, Mexico and the United States signed the Treaty of Guadalupe Hidalgo and ended the war. Mexico agreed to sell the US government 525,000 square miles (1.4 million square kilometers) of land for $15 million (equal to $441 million today). The United

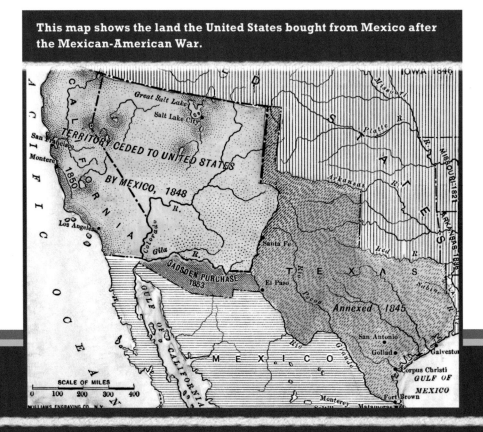

This map shows the land the United States bought from Mexico after the Mexican-American War.

States gained ownership of Texas, Arizona, New Mexico, and California, as well as parts of Utah, Nevada, and Colorado.

There's Gold in Those Hills

Even though California was part of the United States, most Americans—even Polk—had no idea of the riches in gold this area had to offer.

The gold had formed millions of years ago, when volcanoes erupted under the sea. Hot magma bubbled up from Earth's crust and cooled into granite. Superhot fluid containing minerals—including gold—filled the cracks inside the granite. Over time, the granite rock became California's Sierra Nevada mountain range.

Over the years, rain and snow eroded the mountains. The thick granite boulders broke into smaller rocks laced with gold. Those rocks tumbled down the rivers that ran from the Sierras. They landed in smaller rivers and streams in the mountain valleys. A fortune in gold waited to be found.

WHY IS GOLD SO VALUABLE?

For centuries, people have valued gold. They have used it for money, art, and jewelry. In 2500 BCE, the ancient Egyptians fashioned necklaces and rings out of gold. In 1091 the Chinese used squares of gold for money. Alchemists in the Dark Ages tried to convert metals into gold to make themselves rich.

Why have people always valued gold? It is not very useful. Gold is a soft metal that bends easily, so it cannot be used to make tools or appliances. Yet it is beautiful. And it is rare. Gold is much harder to find than metals like iron or copper. It also does not tarnish like other metals. A piece of gold jewelry made a thousand years ago still glitters.

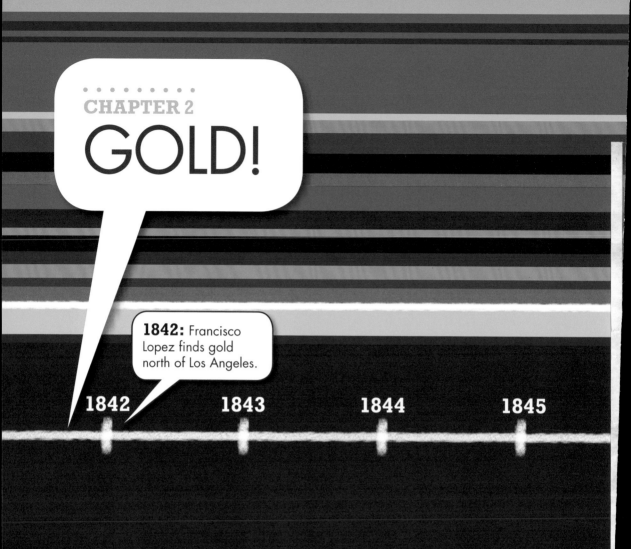

CHAPTER 2

GOLD!

1842: Francisco Lopez finds gold north of Los Angeles.

1842   **1843**   **1844**   **1845**

Just one week before California became part of the United States, a carpenter named James Marshall made a discovery there that would change the course of American history. Marshall was building a sawmill along the south fork of the American River in the Sacramento Valley. The sawmill belonged to his boss, Captain John Sutter. Sutter owned a large fort in the valley about 40 miles (64 km) north. He needed a sawmill to cut logs into lumber for building homes and other new structures.

Sutter and his men had dug a narrow channel to divert water from the river. This water would power the sawmill. On the afternoon of January 24, 1848, Marshall was inspecting the new channel. When he looked down into the shallow water, he saw something shiny under its surface. It was a group of several

Mar. 15, 1848: A story about Marshall's find is published in the *San Francisco Californian* newspaper.

Jan. 24, 1848: James Marshall discovers gold on the south fork of the American River.

Apr. 1, 1848: Another story about the gold find appears in the *California Star* newspaper.

1846 **1847** **1848** **1849**

May 12, 1848: Businessman Sam Brannan announces the find and shows off real gold in San Francisco.

small rocks. Marshall picked them up. The rocks glittered like gold in his hand. Were they really gold?

Is It Gold?

Marshall ran back to the mill to show the workers what he'd found. They were skeptical. They did not believe he had discovered gold.

Marshall wrapped the small rocks in a piece of cotton cloth. He jumped on his horse and rode to Sutter's Fort. At the fort, Marshall found Sutter in his office.

James Marshall

Marshall asked Sutter to close and lock the door, and then showed Sutter the rocks.

The two men looked at an encyclopedia to see if the description of gold matched the rocks Marshall had found. Then the men did a few experiments. They dropped nitric acid on the metal to see if it tarnished. It did not. They compared its weight with silver. It was heavier than silver. They hammered the metal to see if it would shatter. It did not shatter. All signs pointed to the same answer: Marshall had indeed found gold.

A Big Secret

Sutter was a smart man. He knew that if word got out about the find, all of his workers would leave him to seek their

James Marshall at Sutter's Mill.

fortunes in gold. So he and Marshall decided to keep the gold a secret—at least until his sawmill was finished.

Sutter also knew that he did not really own the land where the gold was found. That land had been given to him while California was still part of Mexico, before it became part of the United States. Sutter did not think the US government would recognize his ownership of the land. If he did not own the land, then he would have no claim on the gold found there.

Sutter made a deal with a local American Indian nation, the Yalesummy, to lease the land on which Marshall had found gold. A lease would allow him to use the land in exchange for payments. Then he sent a letter to Richard Barnes Mason, California's military governor, to get the lease approved. Mason said no. The American government did not recognize American Indians' right to lease land.

CAPTAIN JOHN SUTTER

John Sutter was born in Germany and grew up in Switzerland. He claimed to have been a captain in the Royal Swiss Guard, but that probably wasn't true. More likely, he gave himself the fancy title.

In 1834 Sutter was in debt. To escape his money problems, he fled by ship to the United States. He arrived in New York City and then traveled west to seek his fortune. In 1839 he settled in California's Sacramento Valley.

California was under Mexico's control. Sutter became a Mexican citizen. He had learned to speak both English and Spanish before he left Switzerland. Sutter convinced California's Mexican governor, Juan Bautista Alvarado, to give him almost 50,000 acres (20,000 hectares) of land at the place where the American and Sacramento Rivers meet. Sutter started his own little town. He had his workers plant crops and herd cattle. And he built a huge fort with thick walls, gates, and gun towers. Sutter called his land New Helvetia, or "New Switzerland."

By then Sutter and Marshall's news was no longer a secret. Sutter's workers had started to tell their friends about the find. Sutter's prediction came true. Within six weeks, all of his workers had abandoned him to prospect for gold.

News Gets Out

On March 15, 1848, an announcement about Marshall's find appeared on the back page of a newspaper, the *San Francisco Californian*. The blurb read: GOLD MINE FOUND. The article suggested that explorers who tried their luck in New Helvetia might strike it rich. Still, people did not take notice. Gold had been found in California before. It had not amounted to much.

Samuel Brannan

About two weeks later, on April 1, another story appeared in the *California Star* newspaper. The newspaper publisher was a local businessman named Samual Brannan. And he had a good reason to promote the gold discovery.

Brannan had opened a store in Sutter's Fort. He planned to open a second store near the sawmill. He knew that a rush of miners into the area would bring him a lot of new business. But he did not want them to come until he'd had time to stock his shelves with all the supplies they would need to prospect for gold. Brannan bought all the picks, shovels, and blankets he could find. He planned to sell them at steep prices once the miners arrived. By late March, a few curious prospectors had started to trickle into the area.

On the afternoon of May 12, 1848, Brannan stood on a corner of Portsmouth Square in San Francisco. He held up a bottle of gold dust, shouting that the gold had been found in the American River. A crowd gathered around him. Brannan had been to Mormon Island along the American River, one of the places where gold had been found. He had seen the gold with his own eyes. His story convinced many who had doubted the rumors. News of the gold discovery was out.

THE FIRST CALIFORNIA GOLD RUSH

James Marshall was not the first person to find gold in California. Six years earlier, in 1842, a rancher named Francisco Lopez had made his own find. Lopez was riding his horse through Placerito Canyon, about 40 miles (64 km) north of Los Angeles. When he grew tired, he curled up under an old oak tree for a nap. After Lopez awoke, he picked some wild onions he found growing nearby. As he shook off the dirt, he saw gold flakes clinging to the onions' roots. He jumped to his feet and shouted in surprise.

Lopez's find led to a small gold rush. A few thousand people came to Placerito Canyon to mine for gold. But after a few years, all the gold was gone and the mines shut down. The real California gold rush would not begin until 1848.

CHAPTER 3

THE RUSH BEGINS

May 1848: Most of the men in San Francisco leave to search for gold.

May 1848: About eight hundred miners are working in the goldfields around the Sierra Nevada.

| JAN. | FEB. | MAR. | APR. | MAY | JUNE |

June 1848: The number of miners grows to two thousand.

After Sam Brannan's announcement in San Francisco, the trickle of curious miners into the Sierras turned into a flood. They bought every pick and shovel they could find along the way, making Brannan a very wealthy man.

By May 1848, nearly all the men in San Francisco had left town. Stores stood deserted. Newspapers halted production. Crews abandoned their ships. Most of the soldiers stationed at the Presidio US Army post deserted. San Francisco was nearly empty. Yet it would not stay empty for long.

As word of the gold find spread through California, the number of eager prospectors rose. In May 1848, about eight hundred miners were working in the goldfields around the Sierra Nevada. In June two thousand miners were at work. By July that number had grown to four thousand.

July 1848:
An estimated four thousand miners have reached California's goldfields.

July 1848:
Governor Richard Mason and Lieutenant William Tecumseh Sherman tour the goldfields and send a report to President Polk.

Aug. 19, 1848:
News of the California gold find is published in the *New York Herald*.

JULY   AUG.   SEPT.   OCT.   NOV.   DEC.

Dec. 5, 1848: Polk announces the gold find at his annual State of the Union address.

Life in the California gold mines

Many of the miners searched for gold in the American River, where James Marshall had made his find. Others explored the Yuba, Bear, Mariposa, and Feather Rivers. The miners put up rows of tents along the banks of these rivers. New mining camps popped up every day.

Fortune Hunters

In the summer of 1848, the rivers around the Sierras held so much gold that just about any prospector could make money—with a little effort. The average worker in the United States earned $1 a day ($29 today). A hardworking miner could empty fifty pans each day and earn $16 to $25 (equal to $470 to $735 today). In a few months, miners had pulled nearly $4 million ($118 million today) in gold from the California hills.

PLACER GOLD

The men who rushed to the foothills of the Sierras were in search of placer gold—small pieces of gravel that had broken free from larger granite rocks during erosion. Miners could find this gold with nothing more than a pick, a shovel, and a pan.

Placer gold in the rivers took the form of dust, grains, or flakes. A hardworking miner could make a good living by collecting an ounce (28 grams) or more of gold dust a day.

The luckiest prospectors found nuggets of gold weighing a few ounces. The average price of gold in 1848 was $16 ($470 today) an ounce. A nugget weighing 5 or 6 ounces (141 to 170 g) could bring a miner a small fortune.

Word of California's gold riches continued to spread. Updates traveled up the western coast to Oregon. Overland travelers carried the news to New York; Philadelphia; and Washington, DC. On August 19, 1848, the *New York Herald* became the first East Coast newspaper to mention the California gold find. Articles also appeared in Philadelphia and Washington newspapers.

Boats carried the news across the Atlantic and Pacific Oceans. Shiploads of eager miners from Europe, Asia, and Australia began to arrive in San Francisco. People also poured into California from the south—Mexico, Chile, and Peru.

Chinese gold miners traveled by ship all the way from Asia before settling in camps along the Yuba and Bear Rivers.

A MINER'S TOOLS

The California prospectors used a few different tools to mine for gold.

The easiest way to separate gold from rocks and dirt was with metal pans made from iron or tin. A miner dipped his pan into the river to cover the bottom of the pan with dirt. Then the miner swirled water around the pan until the dirt spilled over the sides. The heavier gold sank to the bottom of the pan and was left behind when all the dirt washed out.

Other miners worked together to use a rocker box *(below)*. With a rocker box, miners could process more gold than with a pan. But a rocker box took three people to operate. The wooden box was mounted on rockers like the ones at the bottom of a rocking chair. The miners poured dirt into the box's top. Then they added a bucket of water. As the miners rocked the mixture, the water washed out the dirt and the heavier gold fell to the bottom.

The Long Tom and the sluice box were longer versions of the rocker box. They increased the amount of gold the miners could collect. But they also took more than one miner to operate.

The Governor's Gold Tour

In July 1848, California's military governor, Richard Mason, wanted to see what all the fuss was about. He and an assistant, Lieutenant William Tecumseh Sherman, visited the goldfields. They met with John Sutter and toured the area of the American River where Marshall first found gold. The two men saw about two thousand white men hard at work in the goldfields. Alongside them were about two thousand American Indians, who had been hired as paid laborers. Mason and Sherman watched as the men sifted through the dirt and rocks with pans, rockers, and cradles to find gold.

Mason estimated that each day the men were digging up $30,000 to $50,000 ($882,000 to $1.5 million today) in gold. He packed about 200 ounces (5.6 kilograms) of gold in a tea caddy, and took it with him as evidence of the riches the miners were finding in California. It was worth $3,900 ($115,000 today).

Richard Mason

Then Mason wrote a report for Polk. It claimed the men who were panning for gold earned more in a single day than a US soldier made in a whole month. On August 30, Mason sent a military officer named Lucien Loeser to Washington with the gold. Just to be safe, Mason then sent a second messenger to Washington two weeks later. He wanted to be sure Polk got his message.

Word Reaches the President

Polk did get both messages, and Mason's report was good news for the president. It claimed the gold find would more

Abraham Lincoln

than pay for the recently ended Mexican-American War. The war had not been popular among Americans. Though it had lasted less than two years, it had cost the United States more than $100 million and claimed thirteen thousand soldiers' lives. An Illinois congressman named Abraham Lincoln had accused Polk of starting the war just to spread slavery to the West Coast. Polk needed to convince the American people that the war had been worth the suffering and loss.

On December 5, 1848, Polk made his annual State of the Union address. He told Congress that an "abundance of gold" had been discovered in California. He promised that California would add more to the nation's strength and wealth than any other area the United States had acquired.

Newspapers printed Polk's speech. The reports claimed that so much gold was loose in California that men could collect it with nothing more than a shovel, a pan, and the strength of their arms. The samples of gold Mason had sent to Washington, DC, were put on display in the War Department Library. Polk's message launched a new wave of hungry gold seekers. Thousands more people from around the world set off to find their fortunes in California.

This quarter-ounce (7g) gold nugget was one of the first pieces of gold James Marshall found at Sutter's sawmill.

CHAPTER 4

TO CALIFORNIA: BY LAND OR SEA

June 1849: Americans traveling by ship around Cape Horn begin to arrive in San Francisco.

JAN.   FEB.   MAR.   APR.   MAY   JUNE

Feb. 28, 1849: The first regular steamboat service launches to carry people from the Isthmus of Panama to California.

By 1849 the California gold rush had reached a feverish pace. Thousands of new gold seekers arrived in San Francisco's ports from across the country and around the world. Between 1848 and 1849, the city's population grew from one thousand to twenty-five thousand people.

One of the largest immigrant groups came from China. Many of these men were seeking a way out of poverty and access to the freedom they did not have at home. So many Chinese people arrived during the gold rush, that by 1860, they made up one out of every ten people in California. Europeans also came to the United States to flee war and famine in their own countries. The Irish migrated in droves to escape the potato famine. It was the worst European famine of the nineteenth century, killing almost one million people.

Aug. 15, 1849: The *San Francisco* sets off for the goldfields from the Boston area.

Aug. 1849: Americans traveling overland by wagon begin to arrive in California.

JULY   AUG.   SEPT.   OCT.   NOV.   DEC.

By 1860 Chinese people made up 10 percent of California's population.

All of these cultures brought with them their native foods, languages, and traditions. The population of San Francisco grew and became more diverse. The sight of Chinese men with long braids and robes, along with the sounds of people speaking Cantonese, French, Spanish, and German, were commonplace on the streets of San Francisco.

The eager young prospectors had a name. They were called the 49ers, after the year many of them arrived in California. (San Francisco's football team was later named after them.) Some of the men who sailed to California were called Argonauts. The name came from an ancient Greek myth about a band of treasure seekers who sailed in a ship called the *Argo*.

In the nineteenth century, airplanes had not been invented. No cross-country railroad existed during the gold rush either. Gold seekers heading to the West Coast had only three options.

GOLD RUSH COMPANIES

Travel to California by sea was costly. The price to sail around South America's Cape Horn was about $150 ($4,400 in modern money). It was as much money as some men earned in a whole year. To share costs, many gold seekers joined companies such as the Boston and California Joint Stock Mining and Trading Company and the Hartford Union Mining & Trading Company.

In 1849 more than one hundred gold rush companies formed in Massachusetts alone. On August 15, a ship called the *San Francisco* set off for the goldfields from Beverly, Massachusetts, near Boston. It carried forty members of the Beverly Joint Stock San Francisco Company. Company ships also launched from New York, Baltimore, and Philadelphia.

Each company had between 12 and 150 members. They all had their own sets of strict rules for the men to follow. Members paid a fee to join. In exchange, they received tools, protection, and a share of the gold profits.

They could travel by ship around South America, by wagon across the country, or by a combination of land and sea transport. All three routes were long and dangerous.

By Sea

Most 49ers took the longest route—a 13,000-mile (21,000 km) sea journey around South America. On the first leg of this route, the boats sailed down the East Coast. They rounded Cape Horn at the southern tip of South America. Then they sailed back up the West Coast to San Francisco. The journey took about six months.

The men sailed in clipper ships, whaling boats, or steamships. The largest steamship, the *Edward Everett*, was named after Harvard University's president. The *Everett* weighed 700 tons (635 metric tons) and could carry 150 passengers. It could reach California from Boston in 174 days.

Gold miners cheer at the arrival of the *Edward Everett* in Sacramento.

Travel by sea was grueling. The oceans could be rough and stormy. Many of the men got seasick. At night they slept in cramped berths. By day they ate rotten food filled with bugs. Most food spoiled easily on long voyages because there was no modern refrigeration. One common food on the ships was called lobscouse. It was a hash made from salted meat, potatoes, and a tough bread called hardtack. Water stored on the ships quickly got stale. The men added molasses and vinegar to the water to make it taste better.

By Land

Gold seekers who traveled by land could choose one of many existing routes west. The Oregon Trail stretched from western Missouri to Oregon. The Santa Fe Trail ran between western Missouri and Santa Fe, New Mexico. And the Mormon Trail took travelers from Nauvoo, Illinois, to Salt Lake City, Utah.

The land route from the East Coast to the California

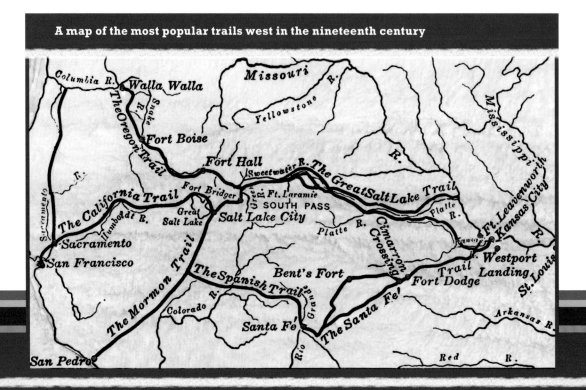

A map of the most popular trails west in the nineteenth century

goldfields was about 3,000 miles (4,800 km). It was much shorter and more direct than the sea route. But the land route was more dangerous.

The oxen-pulled wagons had to lumber across dusty plains, through hot deserts, and over steep mountains. Travelers needed to time their trips carefully to arrive in California before winter. When the weather grew cold, there would be no grass along the trail for their oxen to eat. Winter snows would fill the Sierra passes, blocking the way across.

Water and food were often scarce. The travelers were always in fear of American Indian attacks, although such attacks were rare. Unclean conditions on the trails led to outbreaks of cholera, a deadly infection. About four thousand of the overland travelers died of cholera in 1849. They also passed the disease to American Indians who lived along the trails, killing thousands of them.

Yet these dangers did not stop the gold seekers, who crowded the trails west. One traveler counted 469 wagons along a 9-mile (14 km) stretch of trail.

FLYING TO CALIFORNIA?

In 1849 it took months to reach California by ship or mule-drawn wagon. An inventor named Rufus Porter came up with a much faster way to get there—a steam-powered airship. Porter claimed his 1,000-foot-long (305-meter) balloon could carry two hundred people from St. Louis to San Francisco in just twenty-four hours. The cost for a ticket was fifty dollars. Porter ran into technical problems and never built his aircraft. But he did go on to found the magazine *Scientific American*.

A Shortcut

The third route cut the gold seekers' travel time by at least half compared to the sea journey around Cape Horn. This course took the men down the East Coast, across the Isthmus of Panama, and then up the West Coast.

First, the prospectors set sail from New York, traveling 2,300 miles (3,701 km) to Chagres, a village on the Isthmus of Panama. The isthmus is a narrow strip of land that connects North and South America. From there it was a 50-mile (80 km) journey across the isthmus. On the first part of this trip, travelers paddled up the Chagres River in canoes. Then they set out by mule for a dangerous ride through thick jungles and up steep mountains to Panama City. Many of the prospectors caught local diseases, such as dengue fever,

Prospectors traveling to California by way of Panama rode mules through the jungle for part of their journey.

cholera, and malaria, along the way. From Panama City, travelers caught a steamer ship for the 3,500-mile (5,632 km) journey up the coast to San Francisco. In 1855 the Panama Canal Railway was constructed, making travel across the isthmus faster and easier.

PROFITING FROM THE GOLD RUSH

The miners were not the only ones who made money during the gold rush. Smart businessmen quickly figured out that prospectors needed supplies. They set up shops that sold flannel pants and woolen shirts to keep the men warm. Shops also sold candied fruit and pickled vegetables. These foods would not spoil while the men were out in the goldfields. To protect the miners, the stores sold revolvers and bowie knives.

Shop owners took advantage of the 49ers' newfound wealth. The merchants raised their prices higher and higher as more miners arrived and demand increased. Prices reached $2 ($59 in modern money) for a pound of sugar. A pound of coffee could cost $4 ($117 in modern money). The price of land also rose. One man had bought a piece of land for the price of a barrel of whiskey. Two years later, at the height of the gold rush, he sold it for $18,000 ($529,000 in modern money).

Some men made their fortunes selling equipment and supplies to the miners. Leland Stanford was one of those who struck it rich. He went on to become governor of California, president of the Southern Pacific and Central Pacific Railroads, and founder of Stanford University. Levi Strauss (right) sold tough canvas work pants to the miners. He later switched from canvas to blue denim and added metal rivets to strengthen the pockets. In the twenty-first century, millions of people wear Strauss's pants, known as Levi's jeans.

CHAPTER 5

CALIFORNIA IS CHANGED

Dec. 31, 1849: The population of California swells to one hundred thousand.

Apr. 22, 1850: California's state legislature passes the Act for the Government and Protection of Indians.

1852: The California gold rush reaches its peak.

1849 **1850** **1851** **1852**

1850: California enacts a Foreign Miners' Tax of twenty dollars.

Sept. 9, 1850: California becomes the thirty-first state to join the union.

1851–1852: Mining companies start to replace the sole prospectors.

Between 1848 and 1849, about one hundred thousand people had come to California in search of gold. With the huge population jump came a need for a formal government to keep order. The people of California asked Congress for statehood. On September 9, 1850, their request was granted. California became the thirty-first state to join the union. Although southern lawmakers had wanted to make California a slave state, slavery remained illegal there.

California in 1850 looked much different than it had just a couple of years earlier. Before the gold rush, the population had mainly been made up of American Indians and Mexicans. In 1850 it was a mix of cultures. Mexicans, Peruvians, Chinese, Germans, Chileans, American Indians, and people of many other nations panned for gold side by side.

1853: Hydraulic mining is introduced.

1856: The California gold rush ends.

1853 1854 1855 1856

People from a wide range of cultures sought gold in California.

Yet all was not peaceful in the goldfields. Many of the 49ers from different parts of the country were prejudiced against one another. Yankees from the Northeast often did not trust southerners. Both the Yankees and southerners often disliked people from Missouri or Arkansas. The people many American gold seekers trusted least were the foreigners and American Indians, whom they tried to force out. White Americans did not want to compete with them for gold or resources.

In 1850 California's government enacted a new law called the Foreign Miners' Tax. Any foreigner who wanted to stake a gold claim had to pay $20 a month ($588 in modern money), a huge sum at the time. The tax was meant to push Chinese, Mexicans, and other immigrants out of the California goldfields.

A young Irish immigrant tries to discourage a Chinese immigrant during the height of the gold rush.

Troubles for American Indians

The people who lost the most in the gold rush were California's American Indians. To them, the 49ers were not brave adventurers. Instead, they were intruders who invaded and damaged Indian lands, enslaving or killing anyone who got in the way of their profits.

In the early days of the gold rush, members of nations such as the Maidu, the Nisenan, and the Miwok worked for pay alongside white prospectors in the goldfields. But soon some white men began to see the American Indians as a source of free labor. Many native children were torn away from their parents and forced to work as slaves for the white miners.

California's government only made the situation worse. In 1850 the state legislature passed an Act for the Government and Protection of Indians. Despite its name, the act did little to protect American Indians. Instead, it made it easier for white men to turn American Indians into slave laborers.

Many of California's American Indians lost their land during the gold rush, and some even lost their lives.

For many 49ers, enslaving American Indians wasn't enough. Many prospectors saw the mere existence of native peoples as a threat to their wealth. Groups of white men frequently hunted down and killed American Indians. Local governments and the California state government paid reward money for these murders.

The gold rush had other lasting consequences for American Indians. Mining operations polluted local rivers, killing off the salmon and other fish the American Indians relied on as food sources. Miners swarmed the lands where native people once hunted. With their hunting and fishing grounds destroyed, many American Indians starved to death. Starvation and violence, combined with diseases that American Indians caught from white settlers, devastated California's American Indian populations. Indians who survived these hardships felt a growing distrust and anger toward white Americans. Meanwhile, some white settlers continued their efforts to control native lands and resources at all costs.

Life in the Mining Towns

Mining camps continued to pop up all over the foothills of the Sierra Nevada. The camps started as groups of tents. Over time, the tents were replaced by huts and other buildings made from wood and brick. Shops, banks, and churches were built nearby to serve the miners' needs. Residents gave the mining towns colorful names like Gouge Eye, You Bet, and Dead Mule Canyon. Many of these towns had saloons and gambling halls. There were even theaters where the miners could catch musical acts.

Life in the gold towns was not easy, though. Conditions were dirty. Miners wore the same clothes every day. The men smelled bad and were infested with lice and fleas. Sickness ran through the camps. The men brought cholera with them from their travels across the country. They got scurvy because they had no fresh fruit to provide vitamin C. Scurvy made their skin bleed and their teeth fall out.

When miners were not panning for gold, they drank, gambled, and fought with one another. Thieves were everywhere, trying to steal a piece of the miners' fortune. The towns had no courts or jails to deal with these crimes. So they made their own justice system. Men who were caught often got whipped or branded. Some lost an ear. Others were hanged for their crimes.

A California gold-mining town in 1852

Last Days of the 49ers

More and more prospectors poured into California. More and more gold poured out of the state. In 1848 nearly $6 million in gold came out of the streams and rivers of the Sierras. In 1849 miners found more than $12 million in gold. As much as $53 million worth of gold was discovered in 1850. Gold was so plentiful that it was traded around the world. It replaced silver as the standard metal for world currencies.

As new miners came, their odds of finding a claim dropped. No longer could a man hope to strike it rich with just a pick and a wash pan. The first 49ers on the scene had already scooped up all the loose placer gold. They left behind the larger rocks that could only be mined by digging deep into the mountain or blasting it open. For that the miners needed big machines they could not afford.

WOMEN ON THE WAY

The 49ers had a few things in common. Most were young and adventurous. And almost all of them were men. In the gold rush towns, there was an average of only one woman for every one hundred men.

A woman named Eliza Farnham from New York wanted to change that. Farnham's husband had died in 1848. So she decided to recruit about one hundred women to go to California. These women would marry miners and share the 49ers' newfound wealth. Farnham's plan did not work out—she could not attract enough women to join her in California. But by 1850, more women started to arrive in the gold rush towns on their own.

In 1851 the grizzled miners panning for gold in riverbeds were no longer a common sight. Big mining companies began to take over the difficult work of mining for the remaining gold. Between 1851 and 1852, thirty-three new mining corporations were formed. Investors poured money into these companies. They could afford new and better tools that could dig deep into the rock or blast it into smaller chunks. One of the most efficient methods was hydraulic mining. It used powerful water hoses to break apart the rocks and free the gold. With this method, miners were able to pull more gold from the rock. In 1852 gold production reached $80 million. It was the peak of the California gold rush.

HYDRAULIC MINING

In 1853 hydraulic mining offered California gold seekers a new and faster method of mining gold from rock. Men sprayed the mountains with very powerful jets of water. The water broke the rock into small pieces of gravel, which washed into channels called sluices. From there, it was easy for miners to pull out the gold.

Hydraulic mining was fast. One man could wash tons of gravel each hour. But it was not good for the environment. The streams of water destroyed mountains. Sediment from the mining ran into rivers and clogged them up. Hydraulic mining was so damaging to the environment that it was banned in 1883.

The Gold Rush Ends

By 1856 much of the California gold had run dry. Even the big mines had nothing more to offer. The wave of new miners slowed. Although some gold mining continued in the state, the gold rush was over.

In just eight years, more than 250,000 men had come to California. A few of them struck it rich. John and Daniel Murphy, for instance, found more than $1.5 million in gold by 1848. These lucky prospectors became wealthy landowners. Others went back home empty-handed.

The gold rush was a big gamble that some people won and others lost. But in their search for gold, those adventurous 49ers transformed California into a booming state. A wave of immigrants introduced many new cultures to the American West. The gold rush led to a commerce boom. New businesses on the West Coast needed a faster and more direct way than wagons or ships to transport their goods across the country. In the 1860s, the first transcontinental railroad was

The transcontinental railroad connected the East and West Coasts of the United States.

built to connect the eastern and western United States.

The gold rush also left its mark on the American Indians of California. Before the miners arrived, these native peoples had made up most of the area's population. During the gold rush, thousands of native people were murdered, or died from starvation or disease. The American Indian population in California dropped from one hundred thousand in 1848 to just thirty thousand in 1868. The gold rush set the stage for bloodshed between whites and native peoples that would continue for many years.

And what about the two men who started the gold rush? James Marshall and John Sutter never found their fortunes. Sutter's land was taken over by gold seekers. He died penniless in 1880. Marshall tried to get the people of California to give him credit for finding gold and starting the gold rush. That credit never came. He also died in poverty.

Other states—including Alaska and Georgia—have had gold rushes throughout US history. But none were as big or had as much impact as the one in California. The California gold rush and the 49ers who drove it changed the course of American history.

Writing Activity

Imagine that it is the summer of 1848. You are a miner who has come to California from another country to find gold. Describe what you would see when you arrived at the goldfields. Before writing, ask yourself these questions:

Where did you come from?

How did you get to California?

Where did you go to find gold?

Who else did you see there?

How did other 49ers treat you?

What tools did you bring with you?

How much gold did you find?

How did taking part in the California gold rush change your life?

Glossary

annex: to add to something

Cantonese: a language native to Canton, an area in southeast China

cholera: a disease that people get from drinking or bathing in dirty water

hydraulic mining: a type of mining that uses very strong jets of water to break apart rock

investor: a person who shares the cost and risk of a company but also shares the company's profits

isthmus: a narrow strip of land between two bodies of water

legislature: people who are elected to make or change a country's laws

mission: a building used by a religious group

placer gold: gold that is found loose in riverbeds or streambeds

prejudiced: disliking people because of their race, religion, background, or gender

prospector: a person who searches an area for gold

sediment: material that settles at the bottom of a liquid

LERNER
SOURCE

Expand learning beyond the printed book. Download free, complementary educational resources for this book from our website, www.lerneresource.com.

Further Information

Aronin, Miriam. *How Many People Traveled the Oregon Trail? And Other Questions about the Trail West*. Minneapolis: Lerner Publications, 2012. Learn more about one of the overland routes west that some miners took to reach California.

Behnke, Alison. *A Timeline History of the Transcontinental Railroad*. Minneapolis: Lerner Publications, 2016. Learn about key events of the Transcontinental Railroad, which came soon after the California gold rush.

"The Gold Rush of 1849"
http://www.history.com/topics/gold-rush-of-1849
Learn more about the California gold rush on this History Channel website.

Grayson, Robert. *California's Gold Rush*. Edina, MN: Abdo Publishing, 2012. Discover the colorful characters and events that shaped the California gold rush.

Journey of the 49ers
http://pbskids.sproutonline.me/wayback/goldrush/journey.html
Follow the three routes the 49ers took to reach California's goldfields.

Library of Congress: Western Expansion and Reform
http://www.americaslibrary.gov/jb/reform/jb_reform_fortyniners_1.html
Follow the timeline of western expansion, including the gold rush.

Oakland Museum: "California's Untold Stories—Gold Rush!
http://www.museumca.org/goldrush
Read the stories of immigrants who took part in the gold rush.

PBS—the Gold Rush
http://www.pbs.org/wgbh/amex/goldrush/peopleevents/p_brannan.html
Find out more about Sam Brannan and other people who shaped the gold rush.

Index

Photo Acknowledgments

The images in this book are used with the permission of: © Superstock/ Getty Images, p. 5; © Look and Learn/Bridgeman Images, p. 7; The Granger Collection, New York, pp. 8, 36, 37; Library of Congress, pp. 9 (LCUSZ621491), 14 (LC-USZ62-137164); 24 (LC-DIG-ppmsca-19305), 41 (LC-USZ62-9889); © North Wind Picture Archives/Alamy, pp. 10, 13, 16, 30, 32; © CORBIS, p. 19; © Reinhard Tiburzy/Alamy, p. 20; © Peter Newark American Pictures/ Bridgeman Images, p. 21; © Art Resource, NY, p. 22; Zoeth S. Eldredge, The Beginnings of San Francisco, vol. 2 (New York: John C Rankin Company, 1912), p. 23; AP Photo/Ben Margot, p. 25; © Hulton Archive/Getty Images, p. 27; © Rischgitz/Stringer/Getty Images, p. 29; ullstein bild/The Granger Collection, New York, p. 33; The Beinecke Rare Book and Manuscript Library, Yale University, p. 35; © Christie's Images/Bridgeman Images, p. 39; The Miriam and Ira D. Wallach Division of Art, Prints and Photographs: Print Collection, The New York Public Library, "Eliza W. Farnham," New York Public Library Digital Collections, p. 40; © Fotosearch/Stringer/Getty Images, p. 42.

Front cover: Peter Newark Western Americana/Bridgeman Images.

Main text font set in Caecilia Com 55 Roman 11/16.
Typeface provided by Linotype AG.